GW00836001

WORKS FOR ORGAN AND KEYBOARD

by

Jan Pieterszoon Sweelinck

DOVER PUBLICATIONS, INC.
NEW YORK

This Dover edition, first published in 1985, contains all the music from *Jan Pieterszⁿ Sweelinck: Werken voor orgel en clavicimbel* (2nd, enlarged edition, edited by Max Seiffert), published by G. Alsbach & Co., Amsterdam, 1943, as Part I of *Werken van Jan Pieterszⁿ Sweelinck/Uitgegeven door de Vereeniging voor Nederlandsche Muziekgeschiedenis.* The table of contents has been newly translated and adapted, and a new Publisher's Note, incorporating information from the 1943 (Dutch and German) text, has been prepared specially for the present edition.

Manufactured in the United States of America
Dover Publications, Inc., 31 East 2nd Street, Mineola, N.Y. 11501

Library of Congress Cataloging in Publication Data

Sweelinck, Jan Pieterszoon, 1562–1621.
[Keyboard music]
Works for organ and keyboard.

Reprint. Originally published: Werken van Jan Pieterszⁿ Sweelinck. D. 1. Werken voor orgel en clavecimbel. Tweede aanzienlijk vermeerderde druk naar de bronnen herzien en opnieuw ingeleid / door Max Seiffert. Amsterdam : G. Alsbach, 1943.

1. Keyboard music. 2. Organ music.
M3.1.S95D7 1985 85-752095
ISBN 0-486-24935-2 (pbk.)

PUBLISHER'S NOTE

Jan Pieterszoon Sweelinck (1562–1621), organist of the Oude Kerk in Amsterdam, may be regarded as a major North European counterpart of his contemporaries Giovanni Gabrieli and Monteverdi, like them bridging the Renaissance and the Baroque at the pivotal turn of the seventeenth century. Composer of over 250 choral works, Sweelinck was also an outstanding writer for organ and instruments of the harpsichord family* as well as a highly influential teacher. In his instrumental works, almost all of which are included in the present volume, he absorbed the achievements of the English virginalists and other keyboard composers, and prepared the way for the North German organ school (composers of the caliber of Samuel Scheidt were direct pupils).

Unlike the choral works, extensively published in Sweelinck's lifetime, the instrumental pieces survive only in widely scattered seventeenth-century manuscripts, no more than four of which are autograph. Some of these manuscripts are in organ tablature, others in notation for the virginals. The first critical edition of Sweelinck's instrumental music appeared in 1894, edited by Max Seiffert as the first volume of a collected works edition (*Werken van Jan Pietersz^{n} Sweelinck*). By the time the same editor brought out the second edition of that volume, additional manuscript discoveries had doubled the number of pages; new in the enlarged 1943 edition (the basis of this Dover edition) were Nos. 4, 7, 10–12, 19, 26, 32–37, 39–51, 53–57, 61, 65–68, 72 and 73, not to mention new revisions to the previously published items. These additions not only made available further music by Sweelinck; the "guest" variations in some of the sets also provided new—or the first known—examples of the writing of eminent pupils of the master.

The present volume contains all the music from the enlarged and revised 1943 edition (*Werken voor orgel en clavicimbel*), retaining Seiffert's division into four sections (pieces playable on either organ or [other] keyboard; pieces for organ; pieces for keyboard; supplement) and his titling of the pieces. All headings and wording within the music in German, Latin, etc.—spelled exactly as in the manuscripts—have also been retained unchanged. Seiffert's division and other headings in Dutch, which appear in the table of contents and on the music pages, have been newly translated into English, except for the ubiquitous "variatie" (= variation) and the ordinal numbers preceding that word ("le" = 1st, "2e" = 2nd, etc.). In pieces 35 and 68, the abbreviations "M.J.P.," "M.I.P." and "M.J.P.S." refer to Sweelinck.

Nos. 1–69 are the pieces Seiffert considered complete and authentic. The Supplement comprises four diverse additional items. No. 70 is considered to be based on a Sweelinck original but badly mangled by the copyist; its title "Capriccio" is most likely not its original designation. No. 71 is an authentic work by the great English composer John Bull, written in memoriam shortly after Sweelinck's death; the fugue by Sweelinck on which it is based is lost, so that Bull's piece was included by Seiffert as the only remaining testimony, however indirect, to musical material that was indubitably by Sweelinck. No. 72 is authentic but incomplete. No. 73 is another version of No. 33.

Omitted from the present volume is Seiffert's long introduction (printed in both Dutch and German) on the manuscript sources and other musicological considerations. To aid the reader and performer, however, we here extract and summarize several important principles of Seiffert's edition that he stated in his introduction:

(1) Although Seiffert extensively regularized and modernized such features as clefs, time signatures and note values, nevertheless in a few pieces he retained the stemless black note head that derives from notation practice for virginal music and is equivalent to a half note in certain situations, particularly as a component of quarter-note triplets (thus, for instance, ♩• = ³♩𝅗𝅥).

(2) An accidental in front of a note affects only notes of the same pitch on the same staff, and only for the duration of the measure in which it occurs. Occasionally an additional natural sign is introduced to avoid ambiguity.

(3) An ornament indication—consisting of two oblique parallel lines above or below a note or crossing its stem—is retained from the (English) manuscripts in which it occurs. The type of trill, mordent, etc. to be executed is left to the discretion of the performer.

(4) A few fingerings in the toccatas are carried over from the manuscripts.

(5) Pieces characterized as being "for organ *or* keyboard" never require the use of the pedal, and, within this group, only in the middle section of the echo fantasias is it absolutely essential to use an instrument with two manuals. Seiffert printed these organ-or-keyboard works fundamentally as they

*The term "keyboard" used in the present volume refers to music Sweelinck wrote for virginals or other types of harpsichord. He also composed a few lute pieces, which are disregarded in the present discussion of his instrumental works.

appeared in the manuscripts, which were based more on virginal than on organ practice; thus, organists will often want to tie consecutive notes of the same pitch, whereas harpsichordists would strike the key twice (as written) in order to prolong the tone.

The state of transmission of Sweelinck's instrumental works —in manuscripts only, and almost none of these in the composer's hand—generally precludes automatic authentication and leaves some legitimate room for doubt. Thus, Randall H. Tollefsen, in his article on Sweelinck in *The New Grove Dictionary of Music and Musicians* (1980), does not accept a number of Seiffert's inclusions. Tollefsen lists Seiffert's (this volume's) Nos. 11 and 61 as anonymous works attributed to Sweelinck, calls No. 45 (as well as No. 70, of course) corrupt, and lists as dubious Nos. 12, 15, 19, 23, 26, 34, 36, 39, 40, 42–44, 47, 49, 50, 55, 57 and three of the variations in No. 54. According to Tollefsen's listing, No. 12 has been attributed to John Bull, No. 23 to Hans Leo Hassler, No. 26 to Jakob Hassler, and Nos. 39, 40, 42, 44 and 50 to Heinrich Scheidemann; Tollefsen states that No. 50 is definitely by Scheidemann, and No. 55 by Henderick Speuy. On the other hand, Tollefsen lists as authentic five instrumental pieces not included by Seiffert: one fantasia (G Dorian), one toccata (Mixolydian), one set of chorale variations ("Allein zu dir, Herr Jesu Christ"—not the same as Seiffert's No. 36), one Psalm setting ("Du malin le mechant vouloir") and one set of secular variations (the "Malle Sijmen" pavan). Dover Publications gratefully acknowledges its use of the *New Grove* in the present paragraph, and also in the table of contents of this volume, to which we have added *Grove's* mode identifications. (Dorian, etc.) of the fantasias, toccatas, ricercar and "praeludium."

CONTENTS

WORKS FOR ORGAN OR KEYBOARD

FANTASIAS AND RICERCAR

ECHO FANTASIAS

TOCCATAS

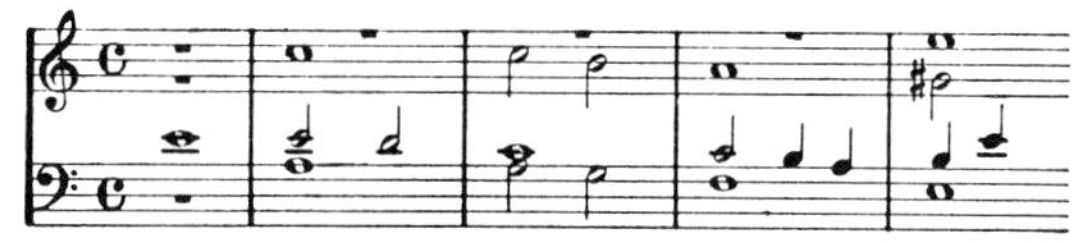

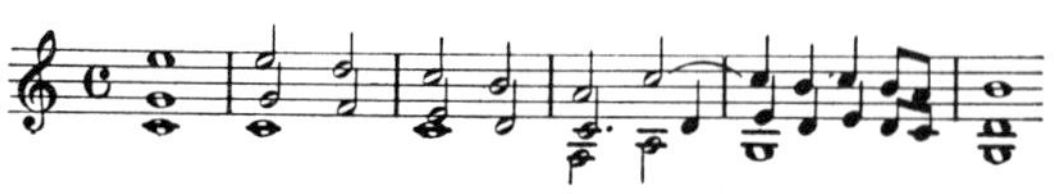

WORKS FOR ORGAN

PRELUDE AND CHORALE VARIATIONS

WORKS FOR KEYBOARD

VARIATIONS ON SECULAR SONGS

VARIATIONS ON DANCE TUNES

SUPPLEMENT

FANTASIAS AND RICERCAR

I. Fantasia Chromatica.

140
150
160

3
3
3
170
3
180
190
3
3
3

2. Fantasia.

70

80

90

100

110

120

240
250
260
270

280

290

300

310

3. Fantasia.

110
120
130

180
190
200
210

220
230
240

4. Fantasia.

80
90
100

5. Fantasia.

60
70
80
90
100
110
120

130
140
150
160

170
180
190
3
3
3
3
3

240
250
260
270

280

290

300

6. Fantasia super: Ut, Re, Mi, Fa, Sol, La.

120
130
140
150
160

170
180
190

200
210
220

7. Fantasia.

60
70
80
90

140
150
160

8. Fantasia.

120
130
140

150
160
170
180

190
200
210
220
230

240
250
260

9. Fantasia.

50
60
70

80
90
100

110
120
130
140
150

160
170
180
190
200

10. Ricercar.

130
140
150
160
170
180

190
200
210
220

230
240
250

11. Fantasia.

80
90
100
110

120
130
140
150

200
210
220
230
240

12. Fantasia ut sol fa mi.

(First Version)

50
60

70
80
90

13. Fantasia.

(Second Version)

110
120
130
140

ECHO FANTASIAS

14. Fantasia.

60
70
80
90
f
p
100

190
200
210
220

15. Fantasia.

50
60
70

16. Fantasia.

30
40
50
60
70

17. Fantasia.

100
110
120
130

180
190
200

210
220
230

18. Fantasia.

50
60
70
80
90
100
f
p

19. Fantasia.

100
110
120

TOCCATAS

20. Toccata.

40
50
60
70

1 2 3 4 3
4
4
4 3
4
80
90

21. Toccata.

50
60
70

80
90
100

22. Toccata.

50
60
70
80

90
100
110

23. Toccata.

50
60
70
80

24. Toccata.

25. Toccata.

40
50
60

26. Toccata.

30
40
50

27. Toccata.

50
60
70

28. Toccata.

60
70
80

29. Toccata.

30. Toccata.

80
90
100

31. Toccata.

70
80
90

32. Toccata.

PRELUDE AND CHORALE VARIATIONS

33. (Praeludium).

34. Ach Gott vom Himmel sieh darein.

1e VARIATIE

30
40
2e VARIATIE a 3
50
60

70
3e VARIATIE a 3
Chorall in Basso
80
(Ped.)
90
100
110

35. Allein Gott in der Höh sei Ehr.

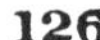

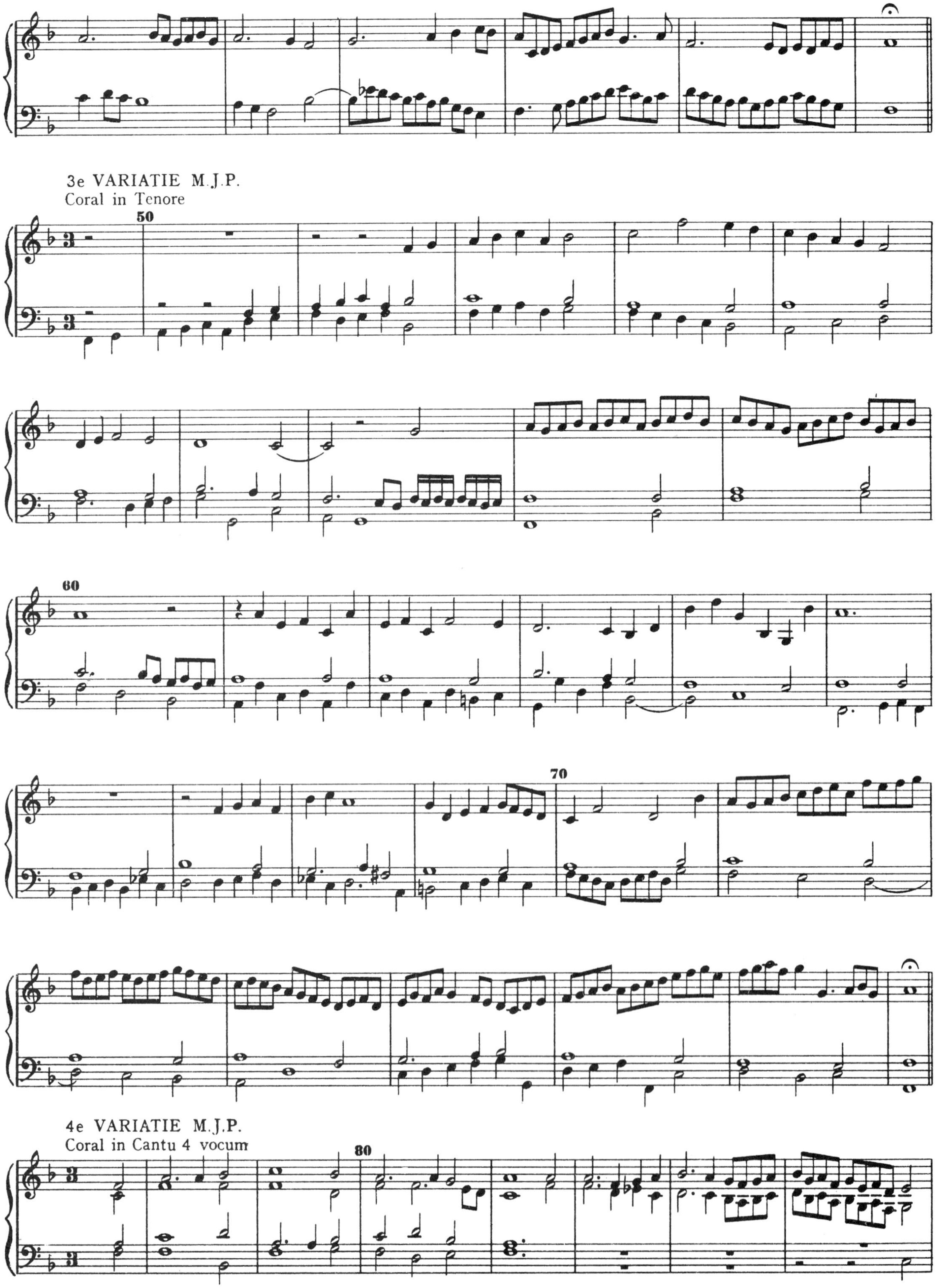
3e VARIATIE M.J.P.
Coral in Tenore
50
60
70
4e VARIATIE M.J.P.
Coral in Cantu 4 vocum
80

90
100
5e VARIATIE A. Duben
Choral in Cantu Auff 2 Clavier
110
120
130

6e VARIATIE A. D.
Choral in Basso
140
(Ped.)
150
160
170
180

7.e VARIATIE A. Duben
Choral in Bass
190
(Ped.)
200
210
220
230

8e VARIATIE [A.D.]
Choral in Bas 3 vocum
(Ped.)
240
250
260
9e VARIATIE [A. D.]
270

280
290
10e VARIATIE P. Hassen
Choral in Tenor 3 vocum
300
1
2
310

11e VARIATIE P.Hass.
Choral im Bass à 3 vocum.
320
330
340
12e VARIATIE G. S.
Bicinium
350
360
370

380
13e VARIATIE G. S.
Choral in Cantu auff 2 Clavir
390
400
410
420

14e VARIATIE [G. S.]
4 vocum

15e VARIATIE [G. S.]
Zum Alt undt Tenor müssen die Stimmen von 4. fuss gezogen werden
480
490
500

510
520
16e VARIATIE [G. S.]
Choral in Cantu auff 2 Clavir
530
540

550
17e VARIATIE [G. S.]
Choral in Tenor
560
570
580
590

36. Allein zu dir, Herr Jesu Christ.

40
50
60
70

37. Christe qui lux es et dies.

2e VARIATIE
Choral Tenor
(Ped.)
50
60
70

3e VARIATIE

38. Da pacem, Domine, in diebus nostris.

2e VARIATIE

3e VARIATIE

4e VARIATIE

39. Dies sind die heilgen zehn Gebot.

40. Durch Adams Fall ist ganz verderbt.

2e VARIATIE
60
70
(Ped.)
80
90
100

41. Erbarm dich mein, o Herre Gott.

2e VARIATIE
(Ped.)

3e VARIATIE
Manualiter vnndt Pedaliter
Man
Ped.
100
110
120

130
4e VARIATIE
140
150

160
170
180

5e VARIATIE
vff 2 Clauier.
Man. I
Man. II
190
200
210

220
6e VARIATIE
230
240

42. Es ist das Heil uns kommen her.

2e VARIATIE

43. Es spricht der Unweisen Mund wohl.

44. Herr Christ der einig Gottes Sohn.

45. Herzlich lieb hab ich dich, o Herr.

50
60
2e VARIATIE
a 4 voc. Coral in Basso
70
(Ped.)
80
90

100
110
120

3e VARIATIE

Bicinium coral in cantu

170
180
190
4e VARIATIE
a 4 voc.

200
210
220
230

240
250
260

46. Ich ruf zu dir, Herr Jesu Christ.

1e VARIATIE
Bicinium: coral in cantu.

40
2e VARIATIE
à 3 voc.: coral in Basso
50
60

70
80
3e VARIATIE
à 3 voc.: coral in Tenore.
90
100

110
6
6
120
4e VARIATIE
à 4 voc.: coral in cantu.
130

140
150
160
170
180

47. Nun freut euch, lieben Christen gemein.

(Was kann uns kommen an - Es ist gewißlich an der Zeit)

1e VARIATIE
Bicinium coral in cantu.

40
50
2e VARIATIE
coral in bas.
60
70

3
3
3
3
80
90
100

48. Nun freut euch, lieben Christen gemein.

(Original Chorale Melody)

2e VARIATIE
Coral Tenor.

3e VARIATIE

Coral Cantu.

49. Nun komm der Heiden Heiland.

1e VARIATIE

40
3e VARIATIE
50
60
70

50. O lux beata trinitas.

1e VARIATIE

2e VARIATIE

Cant.: Coral

51. Psalm 116.

(J'ayme mon Dieu, car lors que j'ay crié)

2e VARIATIE
a 3

3e VARIATIE
Auf 2 Clauiren.

4e VARIATIE
110
120
130

52. Psalm 140.

(O Dieu, donne moy delivrance)

40
50
3e VARIATIE
60

70
4e VARIATIE
80
90
100
110
5e VARIATIE

120
130
3
3
3
3
140

53. Puer nobis nascitur.

3e VARIATIE
30
4e VARIATIE
40
50

54. Vater unser im Himmelreich.

2e VARIATIE
a 4 Voc. coral in cantu

3e VARIATIE
a 4 voc. coral in cantu colloratus

4e VARIATIE

a 4 voc. coral in Basso colloratus

55. Wie nach einem Wasserquelle.

(Ainsi qu'on oit le cerf bruire-Freu dich sehr, o meine Seele.)

30
40

56. Wir glauben all an einen Gott.

50
60
2e VARIATIE
Choral in discant
70

80
90
100
110

120
130
3e VARIATIE
Choral in Tenor
140

150
160
170
180

190
200
4e VARIATIE
Choral in Basso
210
220

230
240

250
260
270

57. Wo Gott der Herr nicht bei uns hält.

2e VARIATIE
40
50
60
70

VARIATIONS ON SECULAR SONGS

58. Est-ce Mars.

3e VARIATIE
40
50
4e VARIATIE
60

70
5e VARIATIE
80
90

6e VARIATIE
100
7e VARIATIE
110
120

59. Ich fuhr mich vber Rheine.

3e VARIATIE
60
70
80
4e VARIATIE
90

100
110
5e VARIATIE
120
130

140
6e VARIATIE
150
160
170

60. Mein junges Leben hat ein End'.

3e VARIATIE
6
6
50
60
4e VARIATIE

70
3
80
5e VARIATIE

90
100
6e VARIATIE
110
120

61. More palatino.

3e
VARIATIE

70
4e VARIATIE
80
90

62. Soll es sein.

3e VARIATIE
50
60
70
4e VARIATIE
80

90
5e VARIATIE
100
110
120

6e VARIATIE
130
140
7e VARIATIE
150

160
8e VARIATIE
170
180
190

63. Unter der Linden grüne.

3e VARIATIE

90
100

4e VARIATIE
110
120
130
140

64. Von der Fortuna werd' ich getrieben.

40
3e VARIATIE
50
60
70

VARIATIONS ON DANCE TUNES

65. Balletto del granduca.

3e VARIATIE
50
60
1
2
4e VARIATIE
70

80
1
2
5e VARIATIE
90
100
1
2

66. Paduana Lachrimae

colorirt.

70
80
90

67. Passamezzo.

50
60
3e VARIATIE
70

80
90
4e VARIATIE
100
110

120
5e VARIATIE
130
140
150

160
6e VARIATIE
170
180
190

68. Pavana Hispanica.

4e VARIATIE S. S.
50
60
5e VARIATIE M.J.P.S.
70
80

6e VARIATIE S.S.
90
7e VARIATIE M. I. Γ.
100
110

8e VARIATIE M. I. P.

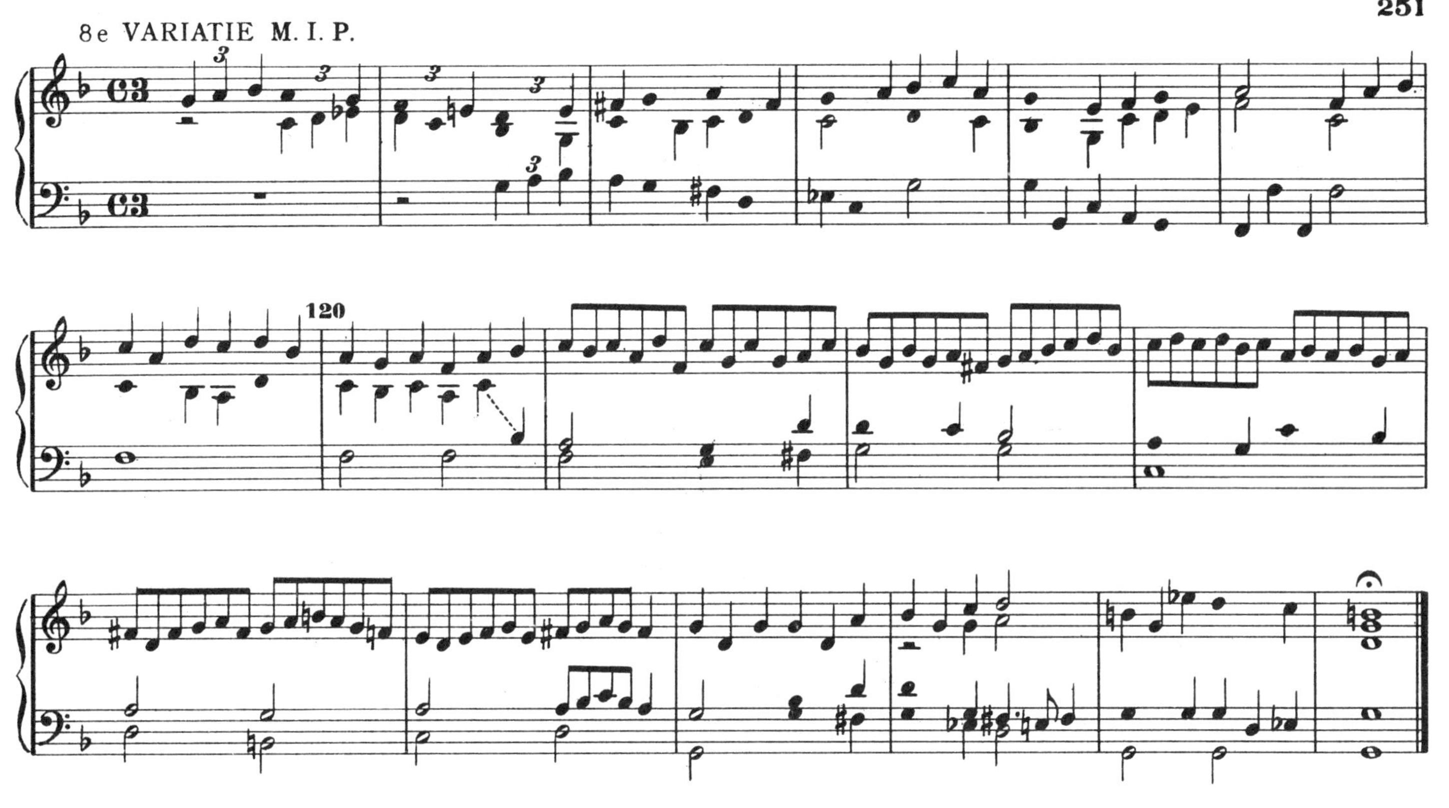

69. Pavana Philippi.

1e VARIATIE

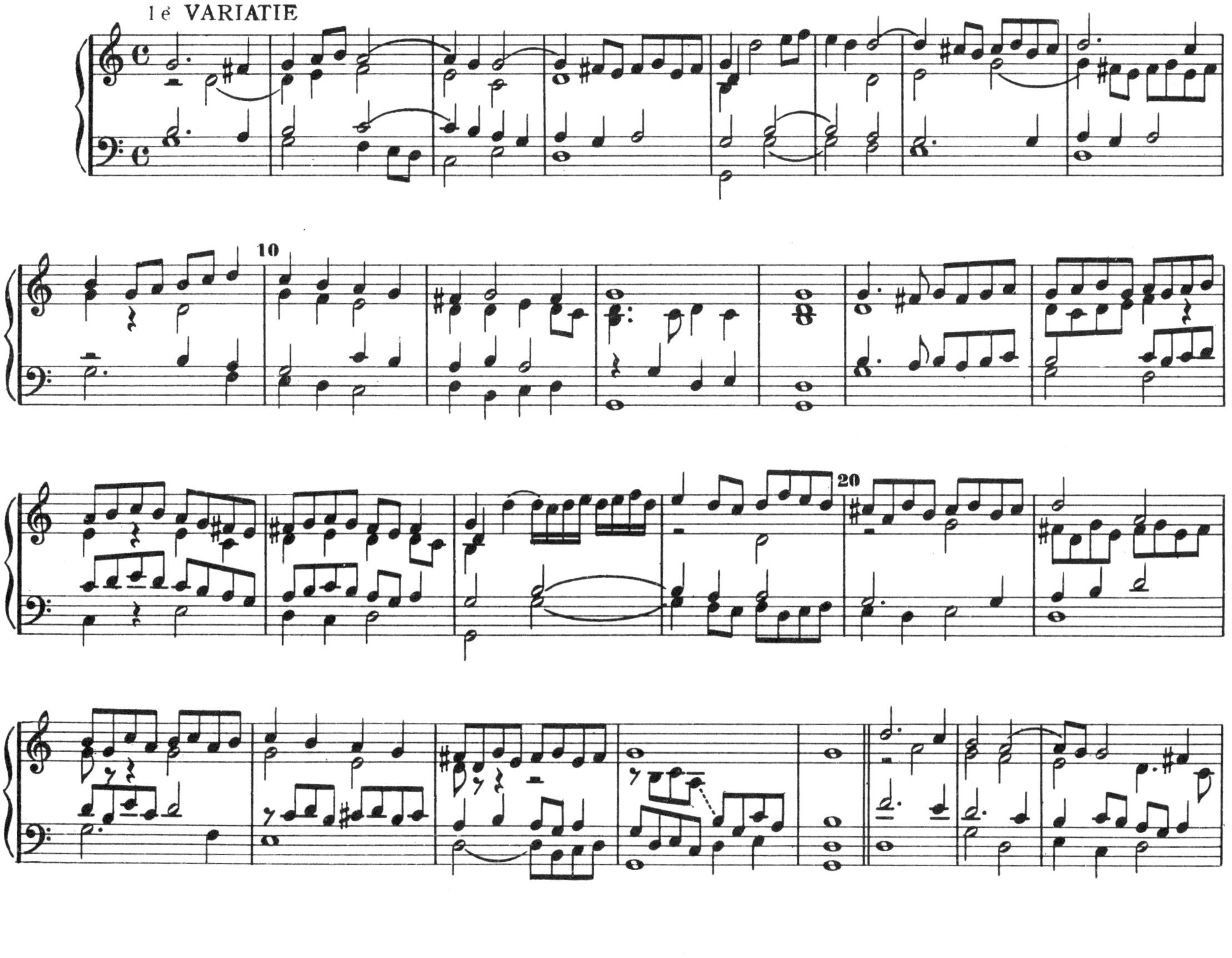

30
40
50
60
70
2e VARIATIE
80

SUPPLEMENT

70. Capriccio.

50
60
70

71. Fantazia op de Fuga van M: Jan Pietersn.

fecit Dr. Bull 1621 15. Decemb.

50
60
70
80
90

72. Toccata.

73. Praeludium pedaliter.